RED-HOT BIKES
DUCATI

Clive Gifford

SEA-TO-SEA

Mankato Collingwood London

This edition first published in 2009 by Sea-to-Sea Publications
Distributed by Black Rabbit Books
P.O. Box 3263
Mankato, Minnesota 56002

Printed in China

Library of Congress Cataloging-in-Publication Data:

Gifford, Clive.
  Ducati / Clive Gifford.
      p. cm. – (Red-hot bikes)
  Summary: "Describes in detail the differences between 6 popular models of Ducati
motorcycles, including statistics for each model and a brief history of the Italian
company Ducati"–Provided by publisher.
  Includes bibliographical references and index.
  ISBN 978-1-59771-135-7
1. Ducati motorcycle–Juvenile literature. I. Title.
  TL448.D8G54 2009
  629.227'5–dc22
                                        2008007313

9 8 7 6 5 4 3 2

Published by arrangement with the
Watts Publishing Group Ltd, London.

Acknowledgments:
The Publisher would like to thank Ducati UK
All images © Ducati Motor Holding S.p.A.

Contents

Ducati—at the cutting edge

In 1926, three Ducati brothers, Bruno, Marcello, and Antonio, formed the Ducati company in Italy. At first, the company produced radios and electrical items. After World War II (1939–45) it started to produce small motorized bicycles.

↑ Leaning into the bend, this rider is testing a Ducati 1098 on the racetrack.

Full throttle facts

Company name: Ducati Motor Holding, S.p.A.
Year of founding: 1926
First bike model: Cucciolo

Employees: 1,134 (2006 figures)
Headquarters: Bologna, Italy
CEO: Mr. Gabriele Del Torchio

Cutting-edge design

Ducati's first biking success was the Cucciolo—a bicycle with a small motor and two-speed transmission. It was sold from 1946 to 1958. Fabio Taglioni joined Ducati in 1954 as a young but ambitious engineer. He became responsible for many of Ducati's cutting-edge designs.

➡ *Fabio Taglioni (standing on the far right) admires the Ducati 750.*

Racing and riding

Over the years, Ducati has grown to become one of the world's leading producers of high-performance motorcycles. They are used on the road and on the racetrack. In fact, Ducati's motto for their bikes is: "Try It On The Racetrack First." Today, Ducati produces a wide range of bikes that all share the company's dedication to styling and superb performance. In this book you will get up close to six of Ducati's most exciting and popular motorcycles.

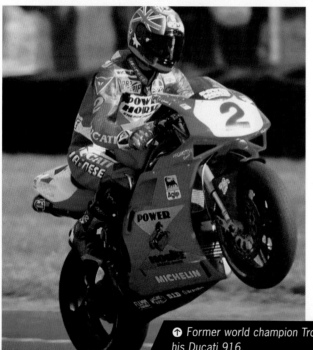

⬆ *Former world champion Troy Corser pops a wheelie on his Ducati 916.*

Number of bikes sold: 35,000
Number of models: 22

Best-selling model: Monster
Number of manufacturing plants: 1

Ducati MTS 1100 / S (Multistrada)

The Italian word *multistrada* means "many roads" in English, and the Multistrada, or MTS 1100, is designed to cover exactly that. It can perform well in many different riding conditions. It is a motorcycle as comfortable on dirt tracks as on regular roads. The MTS comes in two models: the standard 1100 and the 1100 S—a sports version.

More power

The first version of the Multistrada was released in 2003 with a 60.5cu in (992cc) engine. Later a smaller bike with a 38cu in (620cc) engine was produced. For 2007, Ducati increased the engine's size to 66cu in (1,078cc). The Multistrada 1100's engine generates 95 bhp, more than some small hatchback cars.

HOT SPOT

Engine configuration

The number of cylinders an engine has, and the pattern they are laid out in, is called the engine configuration. Ducati builds many of its engines with two cylinders, known as twins. The layout of these cylinders varies. The MTS 1100 has its cylinders arranged at a 90-degree angle, called a V-twin (or L-twin) configuration.

⬆ *The Multistrada 1100 handles winding mountain roads easily.*

Full throttle facts

Top speed: 134mph (215km/h)
Wheelbase: 4ft 9in (1,462mm)

Power output: 95 bhp
Fuel capacity: 5.2 gallons (20 liters)

The Multistrada 620 out on the open road. The bike features an upright riding style, which is comfortable for touring and riding the machine over long distances.

Tech talk

Chassis—the basic frame of a vehicle to which all other parts are attached.

Cylinders—the parts of the engine where fuel and air are ignited to produce power.

Fuel capacity—the maximum amount of fuel that can be held by the fuel tank.

The chassis of the Ducati MTS 1100 is made of tubular steel. This makes the bike very strong and reduces the bike's weight

Here a Multistrada 1100 has been stripped down to reveal its frame, which is made of tough, tubular steel.

Curb weight: 432lb (196kg)
Seat height: 2ft 9in (850mm

Engine capacity: 65.7cu in (1,078cc)
Transmission: 6-speed

Rider comfort

Vibrations from the wheels rolling over a road or track can travel up through many motorcycles' frames. These jolt the rider's hands on the handlebars. Over a long distance this can make riding very tiring. Both the Multistrada 1100 S and the 1100 feature vibration-isolated handlebars to reduce this movement. The bodywork of the front of the bike is split into two sections. A lower fairing covers the front of the bike and holds the front headlight. The upper part is a windshield that turns with the handlebars, offering the rider wind protection when traveling at high speeds.

⬆ *You can see the windshield above the front fairing in this photo.*

MTS 1100 / S (Multistrada)

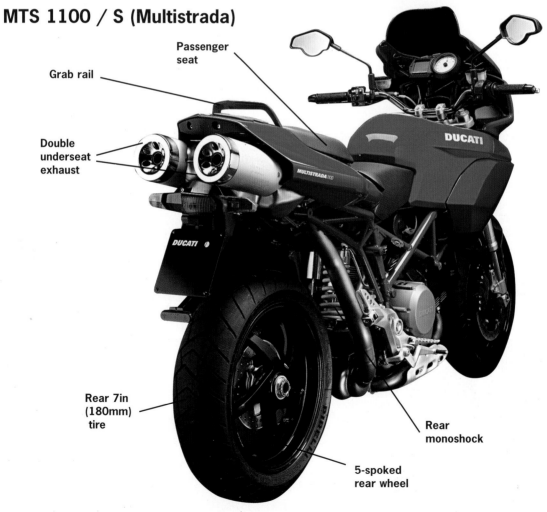

Grab rail

Passenger seat

Double underseat exhaust

Rear 7in (180mm) tire

Rear monoshock

5-spoked rear wheel

Shock absorbers

Shock absorbers are adjustable cylinders connected to the wheel axles. They travel up and down as the bike moves, absorbing some of the shock or impact of riding over dips, ruts, or bumps. The Multistrada 1100 features a pair of front shock absorbers and a single shock absorber, known as a monoshock, for the rear wheel. This rear shock absorber is adjustable depending on the load the bike is carrying and the riding conditions.

Tech talk

Axle—the central shaft that a wheel spins around.

Fairing—a shell, usually made of plastic or fiberglass, fitted over the frame of some motorcycles to direct the air around the bike and rider.

Trellis—a strong, crisscross pattern.

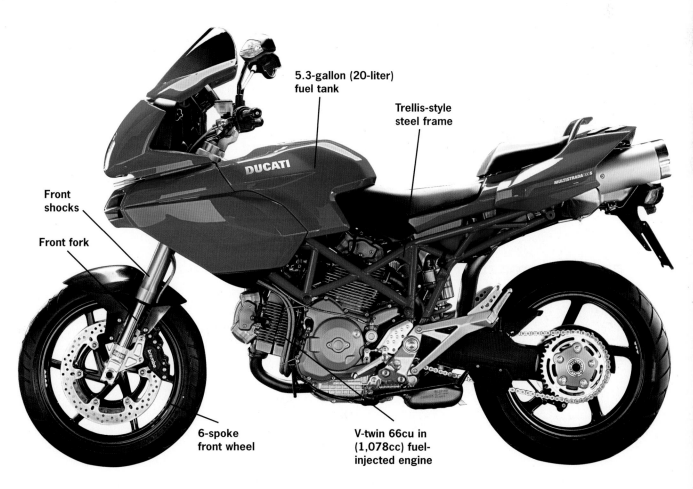

5.3-gallon (20-liter) fuel tank

Trellis-style steel frame

Front shocks

Front fork

6-spoke front wheel

V-twin 66cu in (1,078cc) fuel-injected engine

Wheelbase measures 4ft 9in (1,462mm)

Ducati 1098

The 1098 is the successor to Ducati's famous 999 Superbike, which raced in the World Superbike Championships up until 2006. It won the title three times. The Ducati 1098 is almost 31lb (14kg) lighter, but comes with an engine that is 6cu in (100cc) larger, and generates around 20 bhp more than the 999 it replaces.

Borrowed from racing

Some of the technology in the Ducati 1098 was developed from Ducati's experiences on the racetrack. This includes the machine's powerful disk brakes and the all new Testastretta Evoluzione engine. It is the most powerful twin-cylinder motorcycle production engine in the world.

This Ducati 1098 (left) is the current World Superbike model. Number 21 is ridden by Troy Bayliss.

Full throttle facts

Top speed: 174mph (281km/h)
Wheelbase: 4ft 7in (1,430mm)

Power output: 160 bhp
Fuel capacity: 4 gallons (15.5 liters)

Clear display

The Ducati 1098 has an instrument panel with no buttons on it. Instead, the large LCD display is controlled by a switch on the handlebars. It shows a range of information, including bike speed, engine speed given in revolutions per minute (rpm), oil temperature and pressure, fuel level, and average speed and fuel consumption. The bike and engine speed can be shown in numbers or as a bar graph across the screen.

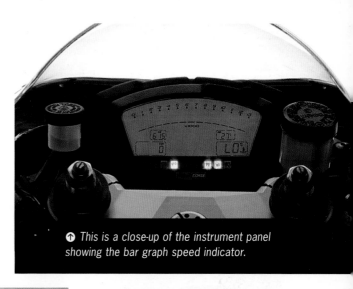

⬆ This is a close-up of the instrument panel showing the bar graph speed indicator.

⬆ A rider takes the Ducati 1098 through its paces. The bike's riding position helps the rider tuck in behind the fairing. This avoids buffeting from the air and helps maintain speed.

Tech talk

Disk brake—a brake system where brake pads press onto a disk attached to the motorcycle wheel, slowing and stopping the wheel from turning.

LCD—liquid crystal display; a type of screen (many flat-screen TVs now use LCDs).

Production engine—an engine built in large numbers for sale in vehicles available to the general public.

Curb weight: 381lb (173kg)
Seat height: 2ft 8in (820mm)

Engine capacity: 67cu in (1,099cc)
Transmission: 6 speed

Sports version

Currently, the 1098 comes in three different versions—the standard model, the 1098 S sports model, and the Tricolore (shown below). The 1098 S is tuned for maximum performance and weighs 4½lb (2kg) less than the standard bike. It comes with a data analyzer package that collects information about the last ride, such as maximum speed and engine performance. This information can be collected by a USB key and put on a personal computer for the rider to check.

↥ *The Tricolore is the 1098 S, finished in a stunning green, white, and red color scheme that matches the Italian flag. It also comes with a racing engine control unit (ECU) and a racing exhaust muffler kit that increases power.*

HOT SPOT

Drive chain

The drive chain is a chain of metal links, similar to a bicycle chain, that transfers the power from the motorcycle's engine to the rear wheel. The chain turns the gear cog, called a sprocket, which is fitted to the rear wheel axle. This moves the rear wheel round.

Ducati 1098

Fuel tank includes a 1-gallon (4.1-liter) reserve tank

Rear light

Twin exhausts made of stainless steel

Front 13in (330mm) brake disk

Rear wheel, with 5 spokes that are Y-shaped for strength

V-twin 67cu in (1,098cc) engine

Drive chain

Rear 9.6in (245mm) brake disk

Twin headlights

Front wheel suspension allows the wheel to travel up and down a maximum of 5in (127mm)

Tech talk

ECU—short for engine control unit, a computer that controls many of the engine's functions.

Muffler—also called a silencer; the attachment at the end of the exhaust system that helps to reduce engine noise.

USB—short for universal serial bus; a way of connecting electronic devices to a personal computer.

Ducati Monster 695

The Monster 695 is the latest version of Ducati's Monster "naked" street bikes. These are bikes stripped of all unessential bodywork, such as the front fairing. As a result, the twin-cylinder engine can be seen clearly.

Monster models

The first Monster, the 900, was unveiled in 1992 at a motor show in Germany. It caused a sensation with its aggressive design. In 1994 Ducati released a smaller model, the 600, and in 1998 they produced the 600 Dark. It had an entirely matt-black finish, allowing owners to customize their bikes. Before the arrival of the 695, more than 170,000 Monsters had been sold internationally.

⬆ *Here you can clearly see the 42cu in (695cc) fuel-injected engine of the Monster 695 on full display.*

Full throttle facts

Top speed: 125mph (201km/h)

Wheelbase: 4ft 8 in (1,440mm)

Power output: 73 bhp

Fuel capacity: 3.7 gallons (14 liters)

Waste reduction

The waste engine gases, or emissions, from the Monster 695 pass through an exhaust system that includes two catalytic converters. Electronic sensors make sure the bike releases as few harmful gases into the atmosphere as possible. The gases finally pass through a pair of oval-shaped mufflers, made of aluminum, which help reduce the noise of the gases leaving the bike (see page 17).

⬆ *The Monster 695 has the lowest seat height of any Ducati currently available.*

Tech talk

Aluminum—a strong, lightweight metal.

Catalytic converter—also called a "cat," this device removes most poisonous gases, or emissions, from an engine's exhaust, before they are released into the air.

Customize—to modify a motorcycle, for example by painting it a different color.

Fuel injection—a system that carefully controls the amount of fuel entering an engine cylinder.

Naked—a class of motorcycle that has very few fairings.

Curb weight: 370lb (168kg)
Seat height: 2ft 6 in (770mm)

Engine capacity: 42cu in (695cc)
Transmission: 6 speed

Cylinders and pistons

When air and fuel are ignited (set alight) in an engine cylinder, the expanding gases created push a piston up and down a cylinder. The movement of this piston is harnessed to drive a motorcycle's rear wheel around. Life for a cylinder piston is fast and furious, pumping up and down at extreme pace and pressure. The engine in the Monster 695 is designed to allow the pistons to travel 17 percent slower than the previous Monster bike, the 620, while not affecting performance. This helps make the engine more reliable.

Monster 695

Front indicator lights

Large front headlight

Front 3-spoke wheel

Front 12in (300mm) diameter twin disk brake

HOT SPOT

Slipper clutch

A clutch is the device that enables gears to be changed when riding. A slipper clutch is designed to slip slightly when a motorcycle rider changes down the gears and brakes sharply. Its aim is to make slowing down safer and more comfortable, and to stop the rear wheel from locking, which might cause the bike to skid over. Slipper clutches are normally found on competition bikes, but the Monster 695 also has one, called an Adler Power Torque Clutch.

Accessories

A range of accessories are available for the Monster 695, including a leather racing outfit and a matching seat cover and fairing set, which can be fitted to the bike. The engine can also be boosted with an engine performance kit. This includes a pair of lightweight carbon-fiber exhaust mufflers, a new air filter, and an engine control unit designed to maximize engine performance.

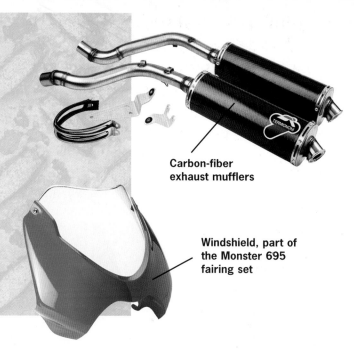

Carbon-fiber exhaust mufflers

Windshield, part of the Monster 695 fairing set

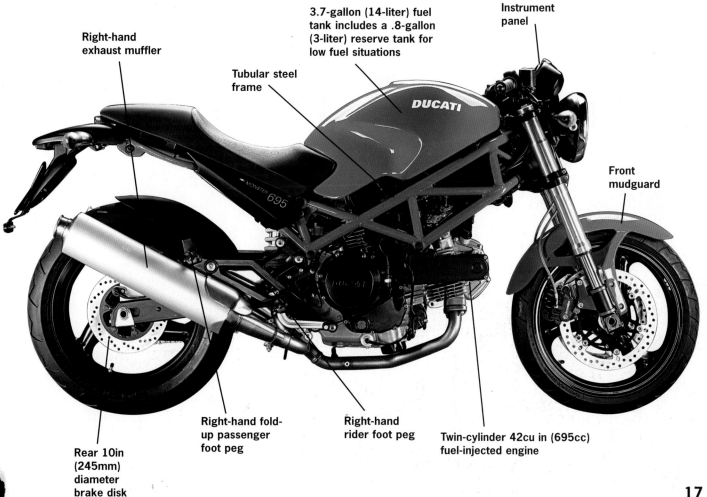

Right-hand exhaust muffler

3.7-gallon (14-liter) fuel tank includes a .8-gallon (3-liter) reserve tank for low fuel situations

Instrument panel

Tubular steel frame

Front mudguard

Rear 10in (245mm) diameter brake disk

Right-hand fold-up passenger foot peg

Right-hand rider foot peg

Twin-cylinder 42cu in (695cc) fuel-injected engine

Ducati ST3 / ST3 ABS

Sports touring motorcycles offer high performance that can be maintained over long distances. Ducati's latest sports touring motorcycle comes in two versions, the standard ST3 model and the ST3 ABS, which features antilock brakes and five-spoke wheels. It also has an upside-down front fork that is fully adjustable for different loads and riding conditions.

⬆ *The Ducati ST3 carries a passenger and luggage comfortably.*

Full throttle facts

Top speed: 150mph (241km/h)
Length: 4ft 8in (1,430 mm)

Power output: 102 bhp
Fuel capacity: 5.5 gallons (21 liters)

Touring traditions

Touring on a motorcycle means long-distance riding and the need for comfort and storage. The Ducati ST3 has handlebars that can be adjusted in height and an advanced on-board bike computer that calculates fuel and range. The exhaust pipes can also be adjusted in height. They can be raised up to allow the rider to lean over further into bends, without the bike body touching the ground. They can also be set to a much lower position, so that the bike can be fitted with a pair of saddlebags for storage.

 HOT SPOT

ABS braking

Sometimes, when a rider applies the brakes hard, the rear wheel may lock and stop turning, and the bike may end up slipping or skidding. Antilock braking systems (ABS) feature sensors that monitor a wheel's speed. A computer determines whether the brakes should be eased off or on for a moment to prevent wheel lock. On the ST3 ABS, the rider can turn the ABS system off for a sporty ride.

Curb weight: 443lb (201 kg)
Seat height: 2ft 8in (820mm)

Engine capacity: 60.5cu in (992cc)
Transmission: 6 speed

Three valve, twin cylinder

The ST3 is powered by the Desmo 3 engine. This is a liquid-cooled, twin-cylinder powerplant with fuel injection. Each cylinder has three valves that help keep fuel consumption low but also allow plenty of power to be generated. When running at 8,750 rpm, the Desmo 3 can generate a hefty 107 bhp.

Cylinders

Ducati ST3 / ST3 ABS

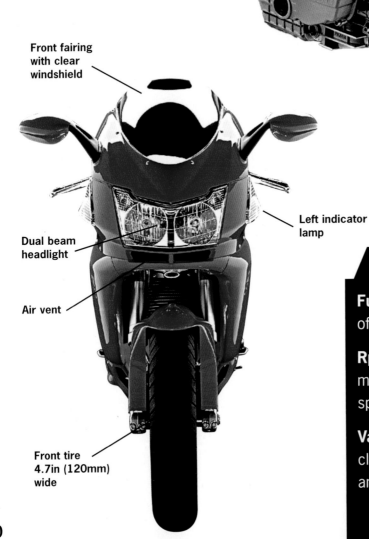

Front fairing with clear windshield

Left indicator lamp

Dual beam headlight

Air vent

Front tire 4.7in (120mm) wide

Tech talk

Fuel consumption—the amount of fuel an engine uses.

Rpm—short for revolutions per minute; a measurement of the speed of an engine.

Valve—a device that opens and closes to control the flow of fuel in an engine.

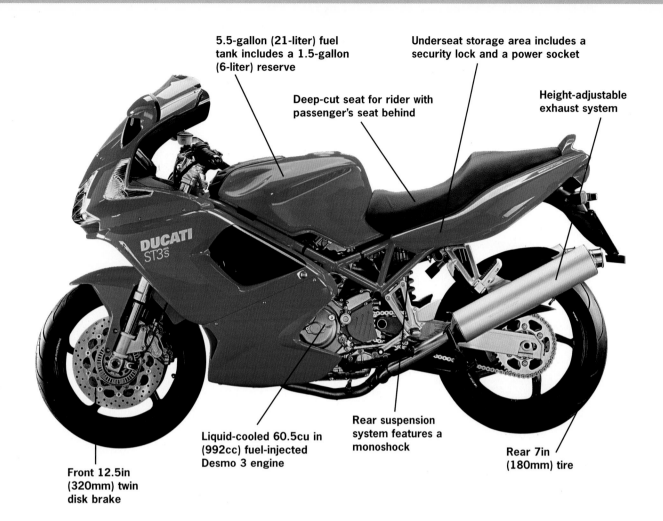

5.5-gallon (21-liter) fuel tank includes a 1.5-gallon (6-liter) reserve

Underseat storage area includes a security lock and a power socket

Deep-cut seat for rider with passenger's seat behind

Height-adjustable exhaust system

Liquid-cooled 60.5cu in (992cc) fuel-injected Desmo 3 engine

Rear suspension system features a monoshock

Rear 7in (180mm) tire

Front 12.5in (320mm) twin disk brake

HOT SPOT

Wet clutch

The clutch is the mechanism that allows a rider to switch up and down gears on a motorcycle. The ST3, like many motorbikes, has a wet clutch system. The moving parts of the clutch are covered in oil. This helps keep their temperature down when the bike is running, as well as reducing wear and tear on the parts. A wet clutch is quiet and hard wearing. It is expected to last well over 62,000 miles (100,000km).

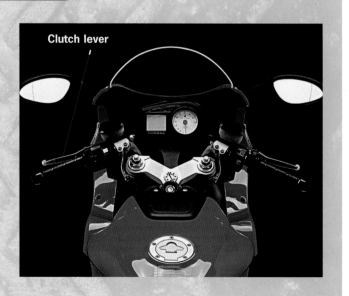

Clutch lever

Ducati GT 1000

In the 1970s, Ducati released a series of GT (Grand Touring) bikes that captured the imagination of many motorcycle enthusiasts. These bikes included the legendary 1971 Ducati GT 750 bike designed by Fabio Taglioni (see page 5). The GT 1000 is a modern classic, designed to capture the spirit of the 1970s.

⬆ The Ducati GT 1000 is a bike designed to look like those from the past, but is packed with modern 21st-century features.

Full throttle facts

Top speed: 134mph (216km/h)
Length: 4ft 8in (1,425 mm)

Power output: 91 bhp
Fuel capacity: 4 gallons (15 liters)

↑ *These riders are making the most of the power generated by the GT 1000's 60.5cu in (992cc) engine.*

Tech talk

Acceleration—an increase in speed of a motorcycle.

Chrome—a silver-colored metal used for its attractive, mirrorlike appearance.

Enthusiast—describes someone who has a strong liking or interest.

Immobilizer—a device that stops thieves from stealing a motorbike by preventing the engine from being started without a key.

Classic styling

The GT 1000 is packed with traditional-looking features, from chrome twin exhausts and spoked wheels to lots of polished aluminum and chrome details. These include the fuel cap, wheel rims, handlebars, and the trim around the instrument panel. The slim fuel tank features depressions called knee cutouts on the sides, which help to create a comfortable riding position.

Curb weight: 408lb (185kg)
Seat height: 2ft 8 in (828mm)

Engine capacity: 60.5cu in (992cc)
Transmission: 6 speed

Fuel efficiency

For a large and powerful motorcycle generating almost 100 bhp, the GT 1000 is relatively fuel efficient. In regular riding it can manage approximately 42 miles per gallon (17.7km per liter). So, a full 4-gallon (15-liter) tank can propel the bike for up to 168 miles (265km). The instrument panel on the GT 1000 includes a trip-fuel function. This allows the rider to check how many miles of fuel are left in the tank.

Ducati GT 1000

Right-hand chrome-covered horn

1970s-style round mirrors

Raised handlebars

Large flat "saddle" seat for rider plus a passenger

1970s-style Ducati logo on fuel tank

Twin rear shock absorbers

Knee cutout

Air-cooled 60.5cu in (992cc) fuel-injected engine

Front 12.5in (320mm) disk brake

Rear 9.6in (245mm) disk brake

36-spoked wheels

Clothing and accessories

To complete the classic 1970s look, a large range of accessories are available for the GT 1000 owner. These include the following:

CAD

The GT 1000 has a classic look, but it is packed with up-to-date features and was developed using computers. CAD is short for Computer Aided Design. It involves the use of powerful computers to shape and design parts on screen, and then run a series of tests, called simulations, to see how the parts and the bike perform. CAD is used to help design many motorcycles, including all those in Ducati's range.

Sportclassic helmet

Monster Dog sunglasses produced by Oakley and Ducati

Leather gloves

Classic-designed leather jacket

Smart boots with toe, ankle, and heel protection

Ducati Desmosedici RR

The Desmosedici RR is the first road-going motorcycle ever to offer the stunning performance and technology taken directly from MotoGP. The RR is a road-going version of the Desmosedici GP7. The GP7 is a new version of the bike that Loris Capirossi and Sete Gibernau used in the 2006 MotoGP World Championship. The attention to detail is so great that this limited edition motorcycle is being produced at a rate of just 400 machines a year.

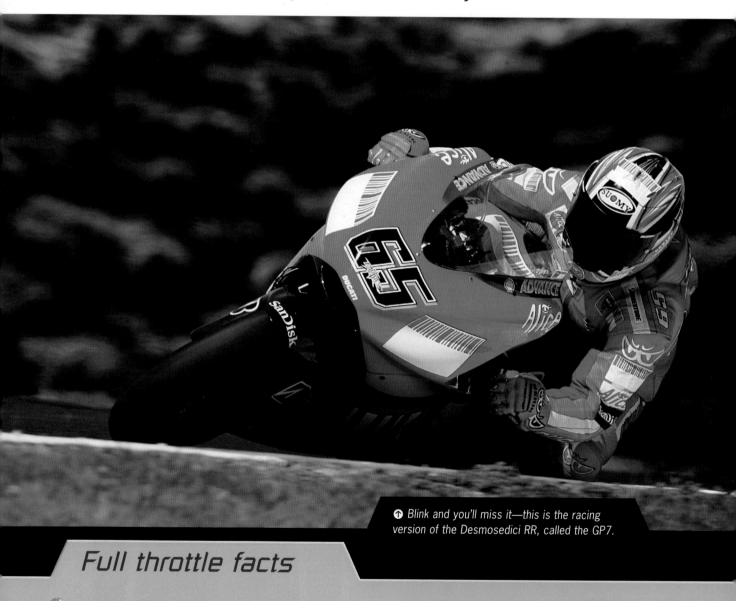

⬆ Blink and you'll miss it—this is the racing version of the Desmosedici RR, called the GP7.

Full throttle facts

Top speed: 211mph (340km/h)
Wheelbase: Information not available

Power output: 200+ bhp
Fuel capacity: 5.5 gallons (21 liters)

Return to MotoGP

At the start of the 21st century, rule changes in Grand Prix motorcycle racing encouraged Ducati to return to the MotoGP competition. The bike they built, the GP3, took part in the 2003 competition. Its successor, the GP4, managed a top speed record of 215.8mph (347.4km/h) when ridden by Loris Capirossi in testing in Spain. In 2006, Ducati motorcycles won four of the 17 MotoGP races, with Loris Capirossi finishing third in the MotoGP World Championship. The latest version is the GP7. It is ridden by Loris Capirossi and Casey Stoner.

⬆ Ducati riders Loris Capirossi (second from left) and Casey Stoner (third from left) pose with team members in front of the Desmosedici GP7 bike in an Italian ski resort.

Curb weight: 364lb (165kg)
Seat height: Information not available

Engine capacity: 60cu in (989cc)
Transmission: 6 speed

Massive power

Most Ducati bikes have twin-cylinder engines. The engine of the Desmosedici RR, like the other Desmosedici machines, features a 4-cylinder engine with an aluminum crank case and titanium connecting rods. This engine can run at staggering speeds. While many bikes can handle 7,000–9,000 rpm, the Desmosedici RR's engine can run at an incredible 17,000 rpm. The engine generates a huge amount of power, in excess of 200 bhp!

HOT SPOT

Desmodromic valves

Ducati's latest high-performance bike is named after desmodromic valves, a technology Ducati has used on their motorbikes since the 1950s. Air and fuel enter an engine's cylinder through a valve, and the exhaust gases leave from another valve. In many engines, the opening of the valve relies on a spring. This can sometimes lead to a drop in accuracy and performance at high engine speeds. Desmodromic valves have no spring, and control both their opening and closing with pinpoint accuracy and smoothness.

Handlebars surrounded by body fairing

Bodywork made of tough but lightweght carbon fiber

Front twin 12.5in (320mm) disk brake

Ducati Desmosedici RR

Tech talk

Alloy—a mixture of metals.

Connecting rods—the rods that join an engine piston to the crankshaft.

Crank case—the metal case that surrounds the crankshaft and rods.

Crankshaft—the shaft in an engine that transfers movement from the pistons to the drive.

Titanium—a very strong, damage-resistant metal.

Fuel tank made of aluminum alloy

Sculpted racing seat, supported by a carbon-fiber frame

A 4-2-1 exhaust system (four pipes leave the engine, one for each cylinder, then run into a single exhaust pipe) hidden under the tail

Rear brake lights

Drive chain

Liquid-cooled 4-cylinder 60cu in (989cc) engine (hidden under fairing)

Bridgestone tires designed especially for the Desmosedici RR

Antilock braking system (ABS)—an electronic system that prevents a vehicle's wheels from locking and improves control when braking hard.

Brake horsepower (bhp)—a unit of measurement used to describe the power generated by an engine that is used to move a bike or other vehicle.

Carbon fiber—a flexible, lightweight material made of strands of carbon that are heated and stretched together.

cu in—short for cubic inches, it is used as a measurement of the size of the engine's cylinders (cc is short for cubic centimeters).

Cylinders—the places in an engine where fuel and air are ignited to generate power.

Drive chain—similar to a bicycle chain, it is a chain that transfers power from the engine to the rear wheel.

Fairing—a shell, usually made of plastic, fitted over the frame of some motorcycles to direct the air around the bike and rider.

Foot pegs—rests or short poles that stick out from the sides of a motorcycles and give riders somewhere to place their feet.

Fuel injection—a device that forces fuel directly into an engine, producing rapid acceleration.

Handling—how a motorcycle responds when being ridden, such as how it turns into and out of corners.

Curb weight—the total weight of a motorcycle with standard equipment and liquids, including oil, coolant, and a full tank of fuel, but not with a rider.

Monoshock—a single shock absorber, found on the rear of a motorcycle, not on the front.

Piston—a disk that moves up and down inside an engine cylinder.

Shock absorbers—devices that are designed to absorb sudden forces and impacts to the suspension of a vehicle.

Suspension—the system of springs, shock absorbers, and other components, directly connected to the wheels or the axles to help create a smooth ride.

Touring—traveling over a long distance.

Wheelbase—the distance between the front and rear axles on a motorcycles.

Further information

Web sites

www.ducati.com
The official web site of Ducati, with information on the latest models and racing performances.

http://drill-online.com/news/
An all-Ducati online newsletter posted by the Ducati Rigers of Illinois (DRILL).

http://www.duc.org/
The worldwide Ducati enthusiast's web site. If you are passionate about Ducatis, the DUC website is the place for you.

http://www.ducatisuite.com/history.html
An interesting look at the history of some of Ducati's most famous and important motorcycles.

Books

The Ducati Story: Road and Racing Motorcycles from 1945 to the Present Day
Ian Falloon (Haynes Group, 2006)
A thorough guide to the company's development and its leading bikes.

Ducati: The Official Racing History
Marco Masetti (Virgin Books, 2005)
A colorful and fascinating look at Ducati bikes in competition, and the technical inventions and innovations that help produce them.

Ducati: The Racing Story
Mick Walker (Crowood Press, 2002)
A comprehensive guide that charts Ducati's racing prowess and success over the decades.

Ducati People: Exploring the Passion Behind This Legendary Marque
Kevin Ash (Haynes Group, 2001)
A book packed with quotes and thoughts of Ducati dealers, owners, and riders as well as technicians who worked at Ducati's factories.

Ducati timeline

1926—The Ducati company forms in Bologna, Italy.

1946—Ducati introduces a 4-stroke 3cu in (48cc) clip-on engine for bicycles, the "Cucciolo" (meaning pup).

1954—Fabio Taglioni is appointed technical director of Ducati.

1955—Ducati's first true racing bike, the Gran Sport Marianna, is developed.

1972—Ducati introduces the V-twin Desmo and the 750 SuperSport.

1980—First Ducati Pantah-engined bike goes on sale.

1989—Fabio Taglioni retires from Ducati.

1990—Raymond Roche on a Ducati 851 wins the World Superbike Championships.

1993—The first Ducati Monster motorcycle goes on sale.

1995—The 916 SBK Superbike debuts.

2001—Ducati MH900e becomes the first motorcycle to be sold only on the Internet.

2003—Ducati bikes totally dominate the World Superbike Championships, winning all 24 races. Ducati reenter the MotoGP competition after a gap of 30 years.

2006—After being owned by Americans, Ducati returns to Italian ownership. Ducati also wins the World Superbike Manufacturers and Riders Championships.